Protect Our Planet

Oceans and Rivers in Danger

Angela Royston

Heinemann
LIBRARY

H www.heinemann.co.uk/library

Visit our website to find out more information about Heinemann Library books.

To order:

☎ Phone 44 (0) 1865 888066

🖹 Send a fax to 44 (0) 1865 314091

💻 Visit the Heinemann Bookshop at www.heinemann.co.uk/library to browse our catalogue and order online.

First published in Great Britain by Heinemann Library, Halley Court, Jordan Hill, Oxford OX2 8EJ, part of Harcourt Education. Heinemann is a registered trademark of Harcourt Education Ltd.

Editorial: Sian Smith and Cassie Mayer
Design: Joanna Hinton-Malivoire
Picture research: Melissa Allison, Fiona Orbell and Erica Martin
Production: Duncan Gilbert
Printed and bound in China by South China Printing Co. Ltd.

ISBN 978 0 431 08476 3
12 11 10 09 08
10 9 8 7 6 5 4 3 2 1

British Library Cataloguing in Publication Data

Royston, Angela
  Oceans and rivers in danger. - (Protect our planet)
  1. Water - Pollution - Juvenile literature
  2. Water quality management - Juvenile literature
  I. Title
  363.7'394

Acknowledgements

The publishers would like to thank the following for permission to reproduce photographs: © Corbis pp.**5** (Christine Osborne), **10** (Richard Bickel); © Getty Images p.**22** (Photodisc); © NaturePL pp.**7** (David Hall), **8**, **14** (Jurgen Freund), **29** (Pete Oxford); © Panos pp.**21** (Chris Stowers), **28** (Martin Roemers), **16** (Rob Huibers); © Pearson Education Ltd p.**26** (Tudor Photography); © Photolibrary pp.**11** (Bruno Morandi), **23** (Cameron Davidson), **25** (D H Webster), **13** (Doug Perrine), **24** (Horst Von Irmer), **9** (Mark Hamblin), **17** (Mike Hill), **20** (Oxford Scientific), **12** (Pacific Stock), **27** (Preston Lyon), **18** (Roy Toft); © Still Pictures p.**15** (Andre Maslennikov).

Cover photograph of a rubbish tip by the coast reproduced with permission of © Getty Images (Raphael Van Butsele).

Every effort has been made to contact copyright holders of any material reproduced in this book. Any omissions will be rectified in subsequent printings if notice is given to the publishers.

Contents

Any words appearing in the text in bold, **like this**, are explained in the Glossary.

What are oceans and rivers?

The sea is the name for the large area of salt water that covers most of the Earth. The sea is divided into five oceans.

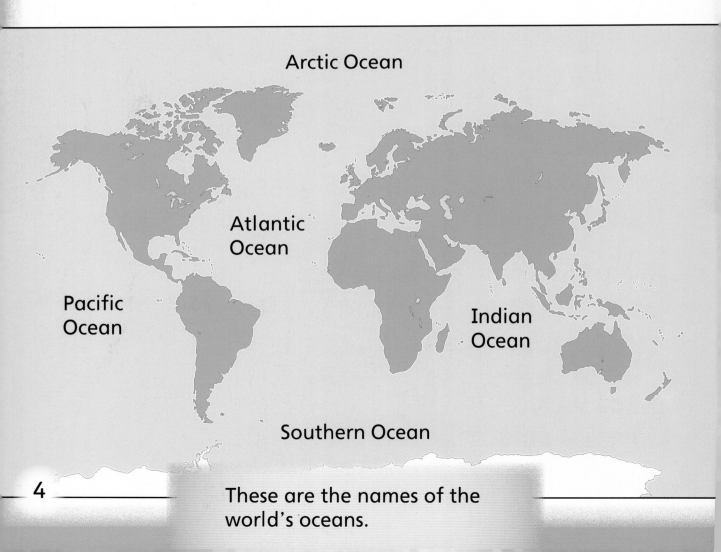

Arctic Ocean

Atlantic Ocean

Pacific Ocean

Indian Ocean

Southern Ocean

These are the names of the world's oceans.

Rivers are large streams of water that flow across the land. Rivers have fresh water, not salty water.

Some oceans and rivers are in danger. They have become dirty because people have dumped **waste** into them.

5

Living oceans

Many kinds of animals and plants live in the oceans. Most of them live in the shallow water around the **coasts**. Many swim just below the **surface** of the ocean.

humpback whale

tuna

mussel

crab

squid

seaweed

shark

green turtle

leopard seal

These are just a few of the animals and plants that live in the ocean.

The water near the surface of the ocean gets the most light. Some sea animals live deep below the surface. It is very dark at the bottom of the deep oceans.

Fishing

People eat many kinds of sea animals. They eat fish, **lobsters**, and other **shellfish**. Most fishermen use nets to catch fish. Fishing boats drag the nets behind the boat.

This full net of fish is being pulled on to a fishing boat.

This seal has a piece of old fishing net caught around its throat.

Fishing nets can hurt large sea animals. Nets that are meant to catch tuna fish sometimes catch dolphins by mistake. Sea animals also get caught in old nets that fishermen have thrown away.

9

Overfishing

The biggest fishing boats can catch huge amounts of fish. In some places there are very few fish left in the sea because so many have been caught. This is called **overfishing**.

Fishing nets catch many fish that are too small to eat.

Fishermen are not allowed to use these boats to fish at sea. They will have to wait a few years until there are more fish.

In some places, governments agree how much of every kind of fish each country can catch. This makes sure that fewer fish are caught. Sometimes one kind of fish becomes so rare, fishermen are not allowed to catch it at all.

Coral reefs

Coral reefs look like rock but they are made of tiny **shellfish**. The shellfish are called **coral polyps**. It takes thousands of years for coral polyps to build up into a reef.

coral polyp

Coral polyps look like flowers but are tiny animals.

Coral reefs grow in warm, shallow water.

Coral reefs are important. Many kinds of fish and other sea animals live around coral reefs. Fishermen catch some of the fish for people to eat.

Damage to coral reefs

Coral reefs are easily damaged. In some places **waste** water from homes and factories flows into the sea. Waste water can have poisons in it. If the poisons reach the coral, the **coral polyps** can die.

Tourists sometimes damage coral reefs when they get too close to them.

Sometimes parts of a coral reef may lose their colour. This is called **bleaching**. Bleaching happens when the sea becomes warmer or colder than usual. If the change in temperature of the sea lasts too long, the coral polyps die.

This is bleached coral.

Pollution in the Sea

In some places the sea and shore are **polluted**. The **pollution** may be waste from factories or **sewage**. It may be litter dropped by people.

Some of the litter on this beach was carried here by the sea.

Oil floats on the water. When it sticks to the feathers of birds, they cannot fly away.

Most people are careful not to pollute the sea. But sometimes there are accidents that cause pollution. Sometimes ships carrying **oil** crash at sea. Then oil spills into the sea and pollutes the **coast**.

17

How are rivers and lakes formed?

Rivers are formed by rainwater. When it rains, the rainwater flows down hills and mountains into streams. The streams join up to make a river.

Rivers flow into lakes and the sea.

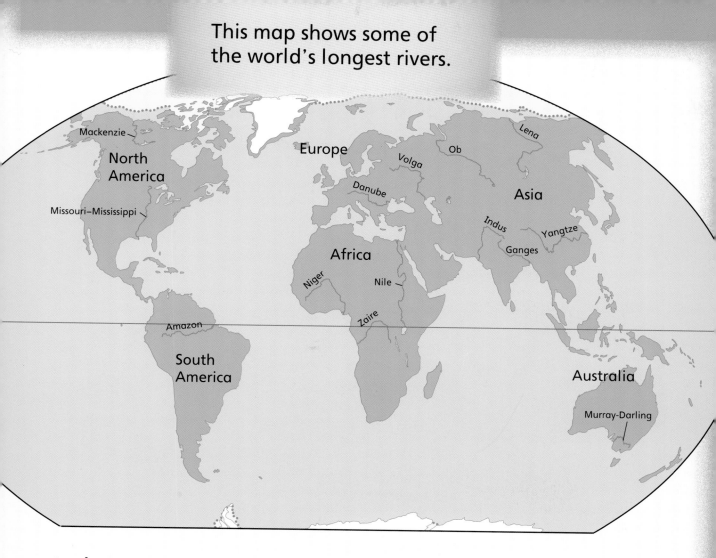

This map shows some of the world's longest rivers.

Mackenzie

North America

Missouri–Mississippi

Europe

Volga

Ob

Lena

Danube

Asia

Indus

Ganges

Yangtze

Africa

Niger

Nile

Zaire

Amazon

South America

Australia

Murray-Darling

Lakes are also formed by rainwater. A lake forms when water collects in a dip in the land. Rivers and lakes have freshwater. Freshwater is not salty like seawater.

Freshwater

Rivers and lakes are important. Fish and other freshwater animals live in rivers and lakes. Almost all the freshwater that people use comes from lakes and rivers.

This brown trout needs to live in freshwater.

This freshwater is being used to water rice crops.

Farmers use freshwater from lakes and rivers to water their **crops**. Water from lakes is cleaned and then pumped through pipes to homes and buildings.

Polluted rivers

Some rivers have become **polluted**. When rivers are polluted, fish and other river animals may die. Some rivers are polluted because **waste** from factories flows into them.

All the fish in this river have died because of pollution.

Some rivers are polluted by the **chemicals** that farmers use. These chemicals make the farmers' **crops** grow better. But some of the chemicals are washed into streams and rivers.

Water from sugar cane fields is washed into this river. Chemicals have turned the water yellow.

Disappearing water

Many rivers and lakes have much less water in them than they used to have. Some rivers dry up completely during the driest part of the year.

This river has almost dried up completely.

The water in this lake used to cover the mud.

Some rivers and lakes are drying up because
people take too much water from them.
Other rivers are drying up because there is
less rain in that place.

Saving water

Many people waste the water that they use in their homes and gardens. People can save water to help stop lakes and rivers from drying up.

Watering plants with a watering can uses less water than a hose.

There are many ways people can save water. Using a bucket of water to wash a car takes less water than using a hosepipe or car wash. People can also save water by having a shower instead of a bath.

Protecting oceans, rivers, and lakes

Many countries have passed laws to protect oceans, rivers, and lakes. These laws stop factories from pumping **waste** into the water.

This scientist is checking the water to see how clean it is.

Some otters are returning to rivers that have become clean again.

Some rivers that used to be dirty are now clean again. Fish and other river animals come back to live in clean rivers.

Plants, animals, and people need water to live. Everyone must work together to protect the waters of the Earth.

29

Glossary

bleaching when something loses its colour and becomes white

chemical substance that things are made of

coast area of land next to the sea

coral polyp tiny shellfish that grows with others in large numbers to form a coral reef

coral reef ridge of hard coral, made of the shells of billions of coral polyps

crop plants grown by farmers to sell or use

lobster large shellfish that people catch and eat

oil liquid found mainly under the ground. Oil is used to make fuel for vehicles and to make electricity.

overfishing when people catch more fish than can be replaced by new, young fish

polluted made dirty by waste

pollution dirt or waste gases or chemicals

sewage waste carried away from toilets

shellfish kind of animal that lives in the water and has a hard shell around its body

surface outside or top part of something

waste things that are thrown out because they are not wanted any more

Find out more

Books to read

Environment action: Save water, Kay Burnham
(Crabtree publishing company 2007)

Reduce, Reuse, Recycle: Water, Alexandra Fix
(Heinemann Library, 2007)

True Books: Environment. Water Pollution, Rhonda Lucas
Donald (Children's Press 2002)

Websites to visit

www.epa.gov/kids/water.htm
This website was created by the U.S. Environmental Protection Agency.
It looks at water and the effects of pollution.

www.water-pollution.org.uk/index.html
This website provides a water pollution guide. You can find out about
types of water pollution, the causes of water pollution, and what you
can do to help. It also has links to other useful sites.

www.water-ed.org/kids.asp
This website tells you about water and how it becomes polluted.

Index